101 Things Every Girl Needs To Know

101 Things Every Girl Needs To Know

101 Things Every Girl Needs To Know   2
Chapter 1: The Fabulous You: Celebrating Your Individuality and Strength   8
    1. The Unique You   8
    2. You Are More Than Your Appearance   9
    3. The Power of Confidence   11
    4. The Importance of Self-Love   12
    5. Accepting and Loving Your Body   13

Chapter 2: Girl Talk: Expressing Your Thoughts and Emotions with Confidence   14
    6. Speaking Your Mind   15
    7. Expressing Emotions   16
    8. The Art of Listening   17
    9. Communicating Effectively   18
    10. The Power of Words   19

Chapter 3: Circle of Friends: Building Healthy and Meaningful Friendships   20
    11. Choosing Friends Wisely   20
    12. Being a Good Friend   21
    13. Navigating Conflict in Friendships   22
    14. Outgrowing Friends   23
    15. Building Your Squad   24

Chapter 4: Confidence is Key: How to Believe in Yourself Even When it's Hard   25
    16. What is Confidence and Why it Matters   25
    17. Cultivating Self-Belief   26
    18. Power of Positive Self-Talk   27
    19. Embracing Failure as a Learning Experience   28

20. Practicing Confidence	29
Chapter 5: Mind, Body, Spirit: Staying Healthy, Happy, and Balanced	**30**
21. The Interconnection of Mind, Body, and Spirit	30
22. Taking Care of Your Physical Health	31
23. Nourishing Your Mind	32
24. Uplifting Your Spirit	33
25. Finding Balance	34
Chapter 6: Brain Power: Unlocking Your Potential for Learning and Creativity	**35**
26. Understanding Your Incredible Brain	35
27. The Magic of Learning	36
28. Embracing Creativity	37
29. The Power of Curiosity	38
30. Nurturing Your Brain	39
Chapter 7: Riding the Emotional Roller Coaster: Managing Your Feelings and Moods	**40**
31. Emotions 101: Understanding Your Feelings	41
32. Emotional Intelligence: More Than Just IQ	42
33. Facing Difficult Emotions	43
34. Healthy Coping Mechanisms	44
35. Seeking Help When You Need It	45
Chapter 8: Navigating the Social Sea: Social Media, Popularity, and Real Life	**46**
36. The Digital Sphere: Understanding Social Media	46
37. Building a Positive Online Presence	48
38. Dealing with Cyberbullying	48
39. Popularity: Not All It's Cracked Up to Be	49
40. Balancing the Digital and the Real	50
Chapter 9: Peer Pressure and Making Decisions: How to Stay True to You	**51**

41. Understanding Peer Pressure	51
42. Say No Like a Pro	52
43. Developing Your Decision-Making Skills	53
44. Defining Your Values	54
45. Your True North: Staying True to You	55

Chapter 10: Oops! Moments: Dealing with Mistakes and Overcoming Challenges — 56

46. Understanding Oops! Moments	56
47. Embracing Your Mistakes	57
48. Learning from Your Mistakes	57
49. Overcoming Challenges	58
50. Resilience: Bouncing Back from Oops! Moments	59

Chapter 11: Your Space, Your Rules: Setting Boundaries and Respecting Yourself — 60

51. Defining Personal Boundaries	60
52. The Importance of Setting Boundaries	61
53. How to Set Healthy Boundaries	62
54. Dealing with Boundary Violations	63
55. Respecting Others' Boundaries	64

Chapter 12: Dream It, Be It: Thinking About Your Future and Career — 65

56. Dream Big	65
57. Discovering Your Passion	66
58. Planning Your Path	68
59. Overcoming Obstacles	69
60. Believing in Yourself	70

Chapter 13: The Beautiful Mosaic: Appreciating Diversity and Encouraging Inclusion — 72

61. Celebrating Diversity	72
62. Understanding Stereotypes	74
63. Encouraging Inclusion	76

64. The Power of Allyship 77
65. The Joy of Unity in Diversity 79

Chapter 14: Power of Kindness: Making the World Better, One Smile at a Time **80**
66. Understanding Kindness 80
67. The Power of Small Acts 82
68. Being Kind to Yourself 83
69. Encouraging Kindness in Others 84
70. The Joy of Kindness 86

Chapter 15: Love, Crushes, and Everything in Between: Navigating Your First Relationships **87**
71. Understanding Your Feelings 87
72. The Importance of Communication 89
73. Dealing with Rejection 91
74. Healthy vs Unhealthy Relationships 92
75. First Breakups 93

Chapter 16: Dollars and Sense: Smart Money Habits for Young Girls **95**
76. Understanding Money: The Basics 95
77. Earning Money: Opportunities and Responsibilities 96
78. Saving Money: Why It's Important and How to Do It 98
79. Spending Wisely: Making Informed Decisions 99
80. Giving Back: The Role of Donating 101

Chapter 17: My Crazy, Beautiful Family: Dealing with Family Dynamics **103**
81. Understanding Family Dynamics: The Unique Puzzle That Makes Your Family 103
82. Accepting Differences: Respecting Individuality Within Your Family 105

83. Navigating Family Conflicts: Learning How to Communicate and Compromise   106

84. Roles in the Family: Understanding and Navigating Them   107

85. Growing Together and Apart: Accepting Change and Evolution in Your Family   109

Chapter 18: Making a Difference: Understanding the Joy of Helping Others   111

86. The Power of One: How You Can Make a Difference   111

87. The Gift of Giving: Discovering the Joy in Helping Others   112

88. Volunteering: Giving Your Time and Talents to Serve Others   114

89. Advocacy: Standing Up for What You Believe In   115

90. The Ripple Effect: Seeing the Impact of Your Actions   116

Chapter 19: Self-Love Sundays: The Importance of Self-Care and Relaxation   118

91. Understanding Self-Care: More Than Just Bubble Baths   118

92. Establishing Your Self-Care Routine: A Ritual of Love   119

93. Mindful Moments: Incorporating Mindfulness into Your Self-Care Routine   121

94. Self-Care and Relationships: Taking Care of Your Social Well-Being   122

95. Overcoming Challenges in Self-Care: When Taking Care of Yourself Feels Like a Chore   123

Chapter 20: Ready, Set, Grow! Preparing for the Exciting World of Adulthood   125

96. Embracing Change: The Journey from Girlhood to Womanhood   125

97. Skills for Independence: Learning to Stand on Your Own   127
98. Navigating Relationships in Adulthood: From Family to Friendship and Love   128
99. Career Exploration: Finding Your Path in the World of Work   129
100. Becoming Your Best Self: A Lifelong Journey of Growth and Self-Discovery   130
101. The Never-Ending Story: Writing Your Own Chapters   132

Chapter 1: The Fabulous You: Celebrating Your Individuality and Strength

1. The Unique You

Have you ever taken a moment to look around and notice how everyone is different? Some people have curly hair, others have straight hair. Some are tall, some are short. Some love to sing, some love to dance, some love to read, and others love to play sports. We are all different in so many ways, and that's what makes us special. That's what makes you special!

You, my dear reader, are unique. You are one of a kind. There is nobody else in this entire world who is exactly like you. You have your own unique combination of talents, interests, and dreams. And you also have your own set of quirks - those little things that make you, you. For example, maybe you love to wear mismatched socks, or maybe you like to eat pancakes with ketchup instead of syrup. These quirks might seem strange to others, but they are a part of what makes you unique, so embrace them!

Being unique is like having your own special superpower. It is something to be proud of. It's something to celebrate. So don't ever let anyone make you feel like you have to change who you are to fit in. Always be true to yourself, because the world needs your unique sparkle.

2. You Are More Than Your Appearance

In today's world, it can sometimes feel like there is a lot of focus on appearance. Social media and television often show images of people who seem "perfect." But it's essential to remember that these images aren't always real. And more importantly, they don't define your worth.

Your value as a person isn't determined by your appearance. It's not about having the perfect hair, the perfect body, or the perfect smile. You are so much more than what you see in the mirror. You are your thoughts, your dreams, your values, and your actions. You are your kindness, your bravery, your creativity, and your intelligence.

Remember, true beauty shines from the inside. It's about who you are as a person, not about what you look like. So don't let anyone ever make you feel like you're not beautiful, because you are - just the way you are.

3. The Power of Confidence

Confidence is like a magical key that can open so many doors. It's not about believing that you're better than everyone else. It's about knowing and believing in your abilities. It's about trusting yourself and not being afraid to step outside of your comfort zone.

With confidence, you can face challenges head-on. You can try new things. You can stand up for what you believe in. It gives you the strength to be yourself and not worry about what others might think.

Confidence isn't always something that comes naturally, and that's okay. It's a skill that you can develop, just like playing a musical instrument or learning a new language.

So don't worry if you're not feeling confident yet. You can start by taking small steps. Try something new. Stand up for yourself. Over time, these small steps will build your confidence.

4. The Importance of Self-Love

Self-love might sound like a trendy buzzword, but it's so much more than that. It's about respecting yourself, caring for yourself, and being kind to yourself. It's about treating yourself as you would treat a best friend.

When you love yourself, you understand your worth. You set boundaries and don't let others treat you poorly. You make healthier choices because you value your well-being. Self-love leads to a happier and more fulfilling life.

It's also important to understand that loving yourself doesn't mean you think you're perfect or better than anyone else. Nobody is perfect, and we all have things we want to improve. Loving yourself means you accept yourself as you are right now, while also striving to grow and become even better.

5. Accepting and Loving Your Body

Your body is absolutely amazing. Just think about it: it allows you to explore the world, to dance to your favorite song, to hug your loved ones, and so much more. So it's very important to appreciate, care for, and love your body just the way it is.

Society often puts a lot of pressure on us to have a "perfect" body. But the truth is, there's no such thing as a perfect body. Everybody is different, and that's okay. What's important is that your body is healthy.

Remember, you are more than your body. You are your mind, your heart, your soul. You are your hopes, your dreams, your passions. So instead of focusing on your body's imperfections, focus on all the wonderful things your body lets you do. And remember to take care of it, because it's the only one you have!

Chapter 2: Girl Talk: Expressing Your Thoughts and Emotions with Confidence

6. Speaking Your Mind

There will be times when you have something important to say, an idea to share, or an opinion to express. Don't hold it in! Speaking your mind is a powerful way to express who you are and what you stand for.

When you have something to say, take a deep breath and speak clearly and confidently. Remember that what you have to say is just as important as what anyone else has to say. People will respect you for having the courage to voice your thoughts and opinions.

It's also okay to disagree with someone else's point of view. Differences in opinion are normal. The important thing is to be respectful when sharing your views and listen to others even when you don't agree with them.

7. Expressing Emotions

Emotions are a natural part of life. We all experience happiness, sadness, anger, fear, excitement, and so many more. It's important to express these feelings instead of bottling them up inside. When you express your feelings, you allow yourself to experience and move through them.

Find healthy ways to express your emotions. You might talk to a trusted friend, write in a journal, create art, or exercise. It's okay to cry when you're sad or ask for a hug when you're scared. It's also perfectly fine to laugh loudly when something's funny or jump for joy when you're excited.

Remember, your emotions are valid. No one else gets to tell you how you should feel.

8. The Art of Listening

Listening is just as important as speaking. When you listen to others, you show them that you value what they have to say. It's a sign of respect.

When someone else is speaking, try to focus on what they're saying. Don't interrupt or start thinking about what you're going to say next. Instead, try to understand their perspective. Show empathy and validate their feelings, even if you don't agree with their viewpoint.

Being a good listener can strengthen your relationships, help you learn new things, and even make you a better friend.

9. Communicating Effectively

Communication is more than just speaking and listening. It's also about understanding and being understood. This includes non-verbal communication like facial expressions, body language, and even the tone of your voice.

Effective communication is about being clear and respectful. If you're feeling upset, instead of yelling or storming off, try to express your feelings calmly. Use "I" statements to express how you feel, such as "I feel upset when..."

Remember, everyone has the right to be heard and understood, including you.

10. The Power of Words

Words are powerful. They can build bridges, heal wounds, inspire dreams, or hurt feelings. Therefore, it's important to choose your words wisely.

Before you speak, think about what you want to say and how you want to say it. Try to choose words that are respectful, kind, and truthful. If you're angry or upset, take a moment to calm down before you speak.

Remember, your words can impact others. Use them to uplift, encourage, and show kindness.

Chapter 3: Circle of Friends: Building Healthy and Meaningful Friendships

11. Choosing Friends Wisely

We meet lots of people in our life, but not everyone can be our best friend, and that's perfectly fine. It's important to choose friends who treat you with kindness and respect. A good friend listens to you, supports you, and is there for you, just like you are for them. They should make you feel good about yourself, not bring you down.

Remember, friendship isn't about quantity, but quality. It's better to have a few close friends who genuinely care for you than many who don't respect or value you. Be open to making friends, but also choose wisely.

12. Being a Good Friend

Friendship is a two-way street. Just as you want to have good friends, you should also strive to be a good friend. Being a good friend means listening, showing empathy, giving support, and being trustworthy. It means celebrating your friend's successes and being there for them in difficult times.

Being a good friend also means knowing when to give your friend space, keeping their secrets, and never judging them for their mistakes. Remember, everyone is human, and we all make mistakes. Being understanding and forgiving can go a long way in strengthening your friendship.

13. Navigating Conflict in Friendships

Even the best of friends have disagreements or fights. It's natural. What's important is how you deal with it. Avoid yelling or blaming. Instead, express your feelings respectfully. Use "I" statements to communicate how you feel. For example, "I felt hurt when..."

Remember, it's okay to take a break if you're feeling too upset to talk. Once you've calmed down, you can discuss the issue more clearly. Always aim to solve the issue, not win the argument. After all, the goal is to preserve the friendship, not to prove that you're right.

14. Outgrowing Friends

As you grow and evolve, you might find that you and some of your friends are drifting apart. Maybe you've developed different interests or your friend is heading down a path you're not comfortable with. It's okay. People change, and sometimes, friendships change, too.

Outgrowing a friend doesn't mean you have to end the friendship harshly. You can let it fade naturally. You might not spend as much time together, but you can still be cordial and kind. Cherish the good times you had together and appreciate the part they played in your life.

15. Building Your Squad

Imagine if you had a group of friends who shared your interests, who uplifted and supported you, and who you could have tons of fun with. Sounds amazing, right? That's what we call your "squad."

Building your squad can take time. Start by being yourself and attracting friends who like you for who you are. Attend social events, join clubs or sports, volunteer, and take part in activities you enjoy. There, you'll meet people who share similar interests.

Remember, in a squad, everyone brings something unique to the table. Cherish the differences as they make your squad vibrant and exciting. Remember to always be supportive and encourage one another. After all, that's what a squad is all about!

Chapter 4: Confidence is Key: How to Believe in Yourself Even When it's Hard

16. What is Confidence and Why it Matters

Confidence, at its core, is a belief in yourself and your abilities. It's about knowing that you are capable, valuable, and worthy, regardless of any setbacks or criticism you may face. Confidence helps you handle pressure, tackle problems, and maintain your mental wellbeing. It allows you to pursue your dreams without letting fear hold you back.

Being confident isn't about being perfect or always feeling strong. It's about having faith in yourself and bouncing back even when times are tough. It's knowing that you are more than your mistakes or your failures. You're a work in progress, and that's okay!

17. Cultivating Self-Belief

Belief in yourself is the foundation of confidence. It starts with recognizing your strengths and abilities. Everyone has something they're good at or passionate about. Identify these areas in your life. Celebrate your achievements, however small they may seem.

It also involves changing the way you think about your weaknesses. Instead of seeing them as failures, view them as areas to improve upon. Remember, everyone has weaknesses, and that's what makes us human. It's how we handle these weaknesses that shape our character and self-belief.

18. Power of Positive Self-Talk

The way you talk to yourself has a significant impact on your confidence. If you constantly tell yourself negative things, you'll start to believe them. But, if you speak to yourself with kindness and encouragement, you'll feel more confident and capable.

Start by becoming aware of your self-talk. Are you often harsh and critical of yourself? If so, it's time to change that. Instead, speak to yourself like you would to a dear friend. Use positive affirmations like, "I am capable," "I am strong," and "I can handle this." Over time, this positive self-talk can help boost your confidence.

19. Embracing Failure as a Learning Experience

Failure can be a big confidence killer. But it's important to remember that everyone fails. It's part of life. What matters is how you handle failure. Instead of viewing it as a reflection of your worth, see it as a learning opportunity. Ask yourself, "What can I learn from this?" or "How can I improve?"

Remember, every failure brings you one step closer to success. It's through making mistakes that we learn, grow, and ultimately become stronger and more confident. So, don't fear failure. Embrace it!

20. Practicing Confidence

Confidence is like a muscle. The more you use it, the stronger it gets. Find ways to step out of your comfort zone and face your fears. This could be anything from trying a new activity, speaking up in class, or standing up for yourself or others.

Another great way to practice confidence is through body language. Stand tall, make eye contact, and smile. This not only makes you appear more confident but also makes you feel more confident.

Lastly, surround yourself with positive, supportive people who believe in you. They can help build up your confidence and encourage you to believe in yourself. After all, confidence is a journey, not a destination. Enjoy the process of becoming a more confident you!

Chapter 5: Mind, Body, Spirit: Staying Healthy, Happy, and Balanced

21. The Interconnection of Mind, Body, and Spirit

The mind, body, and spirit are intricately linked, each affecting the other. Mental and emotional stress can lead to physical illness, and physical illness can lead to mental distress. A healthy lifestyle nourishes all three aspects, leading to overall well being.

To understand this connection, imagine your mind, body, and spirit as a triangle. Each side depends on the other two for stability. If one side weakens, the whole structure is affected. The key to maintaining this balance is self-care, which involves nurturing your mind, caring for your body, and uplifting your spirit.

22. Taking Care of Your Physical Health

Your body is your vehicle in life, and taking care of it is crucial. This means eating a balanced diet rich in fruits, vegetables, and whole grains. Regular exercise, whether it's sports, dancing, yoga, or even walking, can have a significant impact on your physical and mental wellbeing.

Remember to hydrate and get enough sleep. Dehydration can make you feel lethargic and affect your concentration. Lack of sleep can lead to mood swings, poor performance in school, and even health problems. Aim for at least 8 hours of sleep each night.

23. Nourishing Your Mind

Just as your body needs good food and exercise, your mind needs stimulation and relaxation. Reading, creative activities, and problem-solving can help keep your mind sharp. At the same time, activities like meditation and mindful breathing can help relax your mind and manage stress.

Avoid negative influences that might affect your mental health, like excessive screen time or negative people. Instead, fill your mind with positive and uplifting content and surround yourself with supportive, encouraging individuals.

24. Uplifting Your Spirit

Your spirit is your deepest self—your innermost thoughts, values, and sense of meaning. Taking care of your spirit involves practices that make you feel at peace, connected, and inspired.

This might involve spending time in nature, practicing mindfulness, journaling your thoughts and feelings, or connecting with something larger than yourself, such as a community or spiritual practice. The goal is to engage in activities that make you feel calm, grounded, and at peace.

25. Finding Balance

Finally, understand that balance doesn't mean equal time to mind, body, and spirit. Some days, you might need to focus more on physical self-care, and other days, you might need more emotional support. Listen to your needs and respond accordingly.

Remember, it's okay to take time for yourself. It's not selfish—it's necessary. By taking care of your mind, body, and spirit, you're equipping yourself to deal with life's challenges and to help others from a place of strength. This balance leads to a healthy, happy, and fulfilling life.

Chapter 6: Brain Power: Unlocking Your Potential for Learning and Creativity

26. Understanding Your Incredible Brain

Your brain is the control center for everything you think, feel, and do. It's constantly working, even while you're asleep, processing information, solving problems, and creating memories. Understanding how your brain works can help you harness its full potential.

While we often think of the brain as one organ, it's actually made up of several distinct regions, each responsible for different functions. For instance, the prefrontal cortex helps with decision making and problem-solving, while the hippocampus is crucial for memory formation. Understanding these different regions and how they interact can help you maximize your cognitive abilities.

27. The Magic of Learning

Learning isn't just about acquiring knowledge for school. It's a lifelong process that expands our understanding of the world, hones our skills, and contributes to personal growth.

When you learn something new, your brain forms or strengthens neural connections. This process, known as neuroplasticity, allows you to constantly adapt, learn, and grow throughout your life. So whether you're learning to play a musical instrument, mastering a new language, or understanding complex scientific theories, you're reshaping your brain in the process!

28. Embracing Creativity

Creativity isn't just about being good at painting or writing. It's a way of thinking that involves being open to new ideas, problem-solving in unique ways, and expressing yourself. Everyone has the potential to be creative; it's not a talent exclusive to artists or writers. You can be creative in how you approach a math problem, how you decorate your room, or even how you find solutions to everyday problems.

Creativity stimulates different parts of your brain and can lead to increased happiness and reduced stress. So, engage in activities that foster creativity. Write, draw, compose music, solve puzzles, or invent new games – the possibilities are endless!

29. The Power of Curiosity

Curiosity is a powerful driver of learning and creativity. It pushes you to ask questions, explore new ideas, and seek out answers. It's what drives scientists to make discoveries, artists to create masterpieces, and inventors to come up with new technologies.

Embrace your curiosity. Ask questions. Wonder. Dream. Explore. The world is full of mysteries waiting to be unraveled, and you have the brainpower to investigate them.

30. Nurturing Your Brain

Just like your body, your brain needs proper care to function optimally. This involves healthy nutrition, physical exercise, adequate sleep, and mental workouts. Foods rich in omega-3 fatty acids, antioxidants, and B vitamins are great for brain health. Physical exercise increases blood flow to your brain, enhancing its functioning and promoting the growth of new neurons.

Sleep consolidates memory and aids learning, so ensure you get enough rest.

Mental workouts involve challenging your brain with new information or tasks. This can be through reading, puzzles, learning new skills, or any activity that requires mental effort. Remember, the more you use your brain, the stronger it gets!

Chapter 7: Riding the Emotional Roller Coaster: Managing Your Feelings and Moods

31. Emotions 101: Understanding Your Feelings

Emotions are an integral part of our lives. They're the color that paints our world, making us laugh, cry, yell, and even surprise ourselves. Understanding your emotions is the first step in managing them effectively.

Emotions are not just happiness, sadness, anger, and fear; there's a whole spectrum to explore. You might feel overwhelmed, relieved, excited, frustrated, or any number of complex combinations. Recognizing these nuances can help you communicate your feelings more effectively and understand others' emotions better.

Remember, emotions aren't inherently 'good' or 'bad'. They're responses to our experiences, signals from our brains to help us understand and navigate the world around us.

32. Emotional Intelligence: More Than Just IQ

Emotional intelligence (EQ) is the ability to identify, use, understand, and manage emotions in an effective and positive way. A high EQ helps you navigate social networks, succeed at school and work, and achieve career and personal goals.

Improving your EQ can lead to better relationships with your friends, family, and yourself. It involves self-awareness (knowing your own emotions), self-regulation (managing your emotions), motivation (using emotions to reach goals), empathy (understanding others' emotions), and social skills (communicating and resolving conflicts).

33. Facing Difficult Emotions

Life isn't always a smooth sail. We all experience difficult emotions like sadness, fear, anger, guilt, and disappointment. It's natural to want to avoid these uncomfortable feelings, but facing them is crucial for emotional growth.

Acknowledge your emotions without judgment. It's okay to be sad, angry, or scared. These feelings are a normal part of life. Try to understand why you're experiencing them, and what they're trying to tell you. Are they signalling a problem that needs to be addressed? Or a boundary that's been crossed? Listen to your feelings. They are your guides.

34. Healthy Coping Mechanisms

When you're going through tough times, it's important to have healthy coping mechanisms. These are strategies that help you manage your emotions and deal with stress.

Coping mechanisms can include physical activities (like yoga, dancing, or running), relaxation techniques (like meditation or deep breathing), creative outlets (like painting, writing, or playing music), or social activities (like hanging out with friends or volunteering).

Avoid unhealthy coping mechanisms like substance abuse, overeating, or self-harm. These might provide temporary relief but will only harm you in the long run.

35. Seeking Help When You Need It

Sometimes emotions can become too overwhelming to handle alone. And that's perfectly okay. It's brave to recognize when you need help and seek it out.

Reach out to trusted adults in your life—be it your parents, teachers, school counselors, or family friends. If you feel comfortable, you can also consider talking to a mental health professional. They can provide guidance and tools to help you manage your emotions effectively.

Remember, it's okay to feel, and it's okay to seek help when those feelings become too much. Everyone rides their own emotional roller coaster, and seeking help isn't a sign of weakness—it's a step towards understanding and managing your emotions better.

Chapter 8: Navigating the Social Sea: Social Media, Popularity, and Real Life

36. The Digital Sphere: Understanding Social Media

Social media has become an integral part of our lives. It's where we connect with friends, share experiences, and explore our interests. But navigating the digital world can sometimes feel like sailing on an uncharted sea.

Different platforms serve different purposes - Instagram for sharing photos, Twitter for quick thoughts, TikTok for creative videos, Facebook for connecting with friends and family. Understanding the nuances of each platform can help you make the most of them.

Remember, what you see on social media is often a curated version of someone's life, not the whole story. Don't fall into the comparison trap. You are more than the number of likes or followers you have.

37. Building a Positive Online Presence

Your online presence is an extension of who you are, a digital footprint that represents your values, interests, and personality. Building a positive online presence can benefit your personal and future professional life.

Think before you post. Always consider if your posts respect your and others' privacy and dignity. Spread positivity and kindness in your digital interactions. Use social media to uplift others and express your authentic self, not to tear people down.

38. Dealing with Cyberbullying

Unfortunately, the internet can also be a breeding ground for bullying and harassment. Cyberbullying can take many forms, like hateful comments, spreading rumors, or sharing embarrassing pictures without consent. It can feel even more invasive than traditional bullying because it can happen 24/7 and reach you wherever you are.

If you're experiencing cyberbullying, don't blame yourself. It's the bully who's at fault, not you. Report the behavior to the platform, block the person involved, and tell a trusted adult. Remember, you're not alone, and there are people who can help.

39. Popularity: Not All It's Cracked Up to Be

Popularity can seem like the ultimate goal, especially with social media's emphasis on likes and followers. But being 'popular' doesn't guarantee happiness or fulfillment. It can even come with its own set of problems, like pressure to fit in, maintaining an image, or dealing with jealousy.

What truly matters is having genuine friendships and staying true to yourself. Strive to be someone you'd like and respect, rather than chasing the approval of others.

40. Balancing the Digital and the Real

While social media can be a great tool for connection, it's important not to let it take over your life. Make sure to balance your digital activities with real-life experiences. Go out with friends, spend time in nature, read a book, pursue a hobby—whatever makes you feel connected and engaged in your own life.

Remember, the digital world is only a part of the social sea. The real treasure lies in the relationships you build and the person you become as you navigate through it.

Chapter 9: Peer Pressure and Making Decisions: How to Stay True to You

41. Understanding Peer Pressure

Peer pressure is when we feel urged to behave in a certain way or make certain decisions due to the influence of our friends and peers. It can range from harmless scenarios, like trying a new food because your friend insists it's amazing, to more serious situations, like being pressured into drinking alcohol or skipping school.

Understanding the concept of peer pressure is crucial. Remember, it's okay to say no if you're not comfortable with something. Your real friends will respect your decisions.

42. Say No Like a Pro

Saying no can feel hard, especially when you want to fit in or avoid conflict. However, it's an essential skill to develop.

It's okay to prioritize your well-being and values over others' expectations.

There are many ways to say no politely yet firmly. You could say, "I appreciate the invite, but I'm not comfortable doing that," or "That's not really my thing, but you guys have fun." The key is to express your refusal with respect and sincerity.

43. Developing Your Decision-Making Skills

Life is full of choices, and as you grow up, you'll face more and more decisions. Developing strong decision-making skills will help you navigate these choices wisely.

Consider the pros and cons, seek advice from people you trust, and most importantly, listen to your instincts. Remember, mistakes are part of the learning process. They help you refine your decision-making skills and grow as a person.

44. Defining Your Values

Your values are like a compass guiding you through life. They shape your choices, behaviors, and reactions to various situations. Defining your values can help you resist peer pressure and make decisions that align with your true self.

Take some time to consider what matters most to you. It could be honesty, kindness, courage, respect, or many other principles. Understanding your values will empower you to stay true to yourself.

45. Your True North: Staying True to You

In the face of peer pressure, it can be easy to lose sight of who you are. But remember, there's only one you in this world, and that's your strength.

Staying true to you means honoring your feelings, beliefs, and values, even when it's tough. It means not being afraid to stand alone if it means standing up for what's right. And it means understanding that your worth isn't defined by others' opinions.

Your journey will be filled with challenges, but remember, every challenge is an opportunity for growth. Stay true to you, and you'll navigate through life's complexities with grace and resilience.

Chapter 10: Oops! Moments: Dealing with Mistakes and Overcoming Challenges

46. Understanding Oops! Moments

Everybody makes mistakes. They are a natural part of life and growth. Making a mistake does not make you a failure; it simply means you are human, learning, and exploring. These "Oops! Moments" can be stepping stones towards success and personal development, but only if we learn to deal with them in a healthy and positive manner.

47. Embracing Your Mistakes

Embracing a mistake doesn't mean that you have to enjoy it, but it does mean accepting that it happened. Instead of trying to ignore it, downplay it, or beat yourself up over it, acknowledge it. Then, consider what you can learn from it. This perspective shift can turn a potentially negative experience into a powerful moment of growth and insight.

48. Learning from Your Mistakes

Mistakes are great teachers. They can show us what doesn't work and guide us towards what might. They can also reveal gaps in our knowledge, skills, or understanding. Every mistake carries within it a lesson. The key is to listen, learn, and apply that learning to future actions. Ask yourself: What could I do differently next time? What did this mistake teach me?

49. Overcoming Challenges

Life is full of challenges. Whether it's a difficult math problem, a fall-out with a friend, or an embarrassing moment in public, challenges can feel overwhelming. However, overcoming them not only makes you stronger but also enriches your life experience.

Facing a challenge head-on with a positive attitude is half the battle. Remain persistent, stay determined, and most importantly, believe in yourself. Seek help when needed, but remember, you are capable of more than you think.

50. Resilience: Bouncing Back from Oops! Moments

Resilience is the ability to bounce back from adversity or failure. It's the mental strength that lets you keep going, even when things get tough. Building resilience can help you navigate through life's ups and downs with grace and courage.

Remember, every time you pick yourself up after a fall, you're proving your strength and resilience. You're showing the world—and more importantly, yourself—that an "Oops! Moment" is not the end of the story but a new beginning. So keep going, keep growing, and keep learning. After all, it's not the mistakes that define us, but how we respond to them.

Chapter 11: Your Space, Your Rules: Setting Boundaries and Respecting Yourself

51. Defining Personal Boundaries

Just like every person has a unique personality, every person also has their unique set of personal boundaries. These boundaries are the limits and rules we set for ourselves within relationships. They could be physical, like not wanting to be touched without permission, or emotional, like not wanting to discuss certain topics. Understanding and respecting these boundaries is a fundamental part of self-respect and self-care.

52. The Importance of Setting Boundaries

Boundaries are an essential part of a healthy relationship. They help you define your individuality and protect your personal space and well-being. When your boundaries are respected, you feel understood, valued, and safe.

Furthermore, setting boundaries helps others understand how to interact with you and what behavior is acceptable.

Remember, it's okay to say "no," and it's okay to protect your personal space, your time, and your energy.

53. How to Set Healthy Boundaries

Setting boundaries is not always easy, especially when you worry about other people's reactions. Here are a few steps to guide you:

* Identify your physical, emotional, and mental limits. What makes you feel uncomfortable or stressed? These feelings help identify what your boundaries are.
* Communicate your boundaries clearly. Make sure the other person understands your boundaries and why they are important to you.

* Give yourself permission to enforce your boundaries. It's not only okay to protect your boundaries, but it's also essential for your wellbeing.

* Be consistent. The more consistently you maintain your boundaries, the more people will respect them.

54. Dealing with Boundary Violations

Sadly, not everyone will respect your boundaries. When someone violates your boundary, it's crucial to address it immediately. Communicate how you feel and what the other person can do to respect your boundaries better.

Remember, standing up for yourself might be difficult, but it is necessary for your self-respect and self-care. Don't allow guilt or the fear of other people's reactions stop you from protecting your boundaries.

55. Respecting Others' Boundaries

Just as you have your own boundaries, remember that others do too. Make a conscious effort to understand and respect the boundaries set by the people around you. It may require patience, understanding, and good communication, but it will lead to healthier and more respectful relationships.

In conclusion, setting and respecting boundaries is all about understanding your values and honoring them. So, stand tall in your space, establish your rules, and don't be afraid to defend them. Your space is a reflection of you, and you deserve to feel safe, respected, and comfortable in it.

Chapter 12: Dream It, Be It: Thinking About Your Future and Career

56. Dream Big

The importance of dreaming big cannot be overstated. Your dreams serve as the bedrock of your aspirations, laying the foundation for what you hope to achieve in your future. Embrace the infinite realm of possibilities that lie before you. Whether you yearn to traverse the cosmos as an astronaut, express your soul through art, save lives as a doctor, or delight the senses as a chef, remember that these dreams are not only valid, but essential. They are the beacons that will guide you through the journey of your life.

Everyone has a unique set of dreams, and it's okay if yours don't look like those of your friends or family. You may dream of building your own business, writing a book, becoming a professional athlete, or inventing something that will change the world. Let your imagination soar without bounds. After all, today's dreams are the seeds for tomorrow's realities.

57. Discovering Your Passion

As you dream big, you'll begin to identify patterns, themes, and areas that resonate with you the most. These are your passions. A passion is more than just a hobby or a pastime; it's a deep, intrinsic interest that fires you up, something you would happily dedicate hours to without expecting anything in return.

Your passion might be in music, science, literature, sports, nature, or any other field. It might be in helping others, solving complex problems, creating beautiful designs, or fighting for justice. To discover your passion, reflect on what truly moves you. Recall the times when you felt most alive, most engaged, and most satisfied. Your passion often lies within these moments.

Recognizing your passion can be a journey in itself. You may have to try different activities, delve into various fields, or experiment with diverse experiences. And that's perfectly fine. Sometimes, the journey of discovery can be just as fulfilling as the destination itself.

58. Planning Your Path

Dreaming big and discovering your passion are the first steps towards your future. But to get there, you need to pave your path with a clear plan. This plan serves as your roadmap, detailing the specific steps you need to take towards your goal.

Start by setting short-term and long-term goals. Short-term goals are like stepping stones that lead you towards your long-term goals. They are easier and quicker to achieve, and they provide regular milestones to celebrate and keep you motivated. Long-term goals are your ultimate destination. They take more time, effort, and patience to achieve, but they also offer the most significant rewards.

Your plan should also consider the skills, knowledge, and experiences you'll need to achieve your goals. What subjects do you need to excel in? What books should you read? What courses or internships should you pursue? Be as detailed as possible in your plan, but also be flexible. Life is unpredictable, and you might need to adjust your plan as you go along.

59. Overcoming Obstacles

Your path towards your future won't always be smooth. You'll encounter obstacles that will test your patience, determination, and resilience. These might be external factors like financial constraints, lack of opportunities, or societal expectations. Or they might be internal obstacles like self-doubt, fear of failure, or lack of motivation.

Overcoming these obstacles might require creative problem-solving, additional learning, seeking help from others, or even some personal transformation. You might have to rethink your strategy, work harder, or cultivate new mindsets. You might also need to practice patience and learn to endure failure and frustration.

However, remember that these obstacles are not meant to deter you but to strengthen you. They provide invaluable lessons and experiences that prepare you for your future. With every hurdle you overcome, you become more resilient, capable, and confident.

60. Believing in Yourself

Perhaps the most crucial element of planning for your future and career is believing in yourself. Without self-belief, even the most well-constructed plan would crumble. Self-belief fuels your motivation, fuels your effort, and sustains your resilience.

Believing in yourself involves recognizing your worth and acknowledging your potential. It involves celebrating your strengths, embracing your uniqueness, and accepting your flaws. It also involves trusting in your abilities to learn, grow, and overcome challenges.

Cultivating self-belief can be a lifelong journey. It requires regular self-reflection, self-affirmation, and self-care. Surround yourself with positive influences—people who uplift you, inspire you, and believe in you. And remember, every setback is a setup for a comeback. So even when you stumble, pick yourself up, dust yourself off, and believe that you can and will achieve your dreams.

Remember, your future and career are not predetermined or fixed. They are shaped by your dreams, passions, plans, and beliefs. So dream big, find your passion, plan your path, overcome your obstacles, and believe in yourself. With these elements, you have the power to shape a future and career that will bring you fulfillment, joy, and success.

Chapter 13: The Beautiful Mosaic: Appreciating Diversity and Encouraging Inclusion

61. Celebrating Diversity

The world is an enchanting mosaic of different cultures, languages, beliefs, and experiences. It's a vast panorama where every person is a unique piece, shaped by a distinct blend of influences and circumstances. Recognizing and celebrating this diversity is crucial for personal growth and global understanding.

By acknowledging diversity, we open our minds to new ideas, perspectives, and experiences. We can learn so much from the customs, values, histories, and wisdom of different cultures. Each culture is a treasure trove of knowledge, experiences, and ideas, and exploring them can enrich our understanding of the world and ourselves.

Similarly, diversity isn't just about culture. It encompasses different viewpoints, lifestyles, abilities, and identities. There's beauty in how every person perceives the world in their unique way. By embracing this diversity of thought and experiences, we can challenge our assumptions, broaden our perspectives, and foster innovation and creativity.

However, appreciating diversity isn't just about celebrating differences. It's also about recognizing and respecting our shared humanity. Despite our differences, we are all humans with the same fundamental needs, desires, and rights. We all long for love, acceptance, happiness, and fulfillment. We all aspire to live a meaningful and rewarding life. Recognizing our shared humanity can cultivate empathy, compassion, and unity amidst diversity.

62. Understanding Stereotypes

As we explore the beautiful mosaic of diversity, it's crucial to confront the shadows that can cloud our understanding:

stereotypes. Stereotypes are oversimplified and generalized perceptions about specific groups of people. They can be about race, gender, religion, nationality, age, profession, or any other characteristic. They can be positive or negative, but they are harmful because they deny the complexity and individuality of people.

Stereotypes can breed prejudice, discrimination, and misunderstanding. They can constrain our thinking, limit our perceptions, and divide us. They can cause us to make assumptions, jump to conclusions, and judge people unfairly.

To break down stereotypes, we need to educate ourselves, question our assumptions, and engage with diverse people. We need to seek out accurate and comprehensive information, challenge biased narratives, and listen to diverse voices. We need to empathize with people's experiences, respect their individuality, and recognize their humanity.

63. Encouraging Inclusion

Celebrating diversity and understanding stereotypes are essential steps towards promoting inclusion. Inclusion is about creating environments where everyone, regardless of their backgrounds, identities, or abilities, feels valued, respected, and empowered. It's about ensuring everyone has equal opportunities, rights, and access. It's about fostering unity in diversity.

Promoting inclusion can start with our everyday interactions. It can involve inviting diverse voices into conversations, making spaces accessible for all, or standing up against discrimination and bias. It can involve appreciating everyone's unique contributions, acknowledging their experiences, and supporting their needs.

However, encouraging inclusion also requires systemic changes. It involves advocating for fair policies, challenging discriminatory practices, and raising awareness about diversity and inclusion. It involves collaboration, solidarity, and collective action.

64. The Power of Allyship

One potent tool for promoting diversity and inclusion is allyship. An ally is someone who uses their privilege to advocate for those who are marginalized or underrepresented. Allyship involves standing up against discrimination, amplifying marginalized voices, and advocating for equality and justice.

Becoming an ally requires understanding your own privilege, educating yourself about different experiences and injustices, and actively supporting marginalized groups. It involves listening, learning, and challenging your biases and assumptions. It involves speaking up, taking action, and stepping aside when needed.

However, allyship isn't about speaking for others or saving them. It's about supporting them, empowering them, and standing with them. It's about acknowledging their strength, honoring their experiences, and respecting their autonomy. It's about being accountable, responsive, and humble.

65. The Joy of Unity in Diversity

The culmination of celebrating diversity, understanding stereotypes, encouraging inclusion, and practicing allyship is a profound joy: the joy of unity in diversity. It's the joy of living in a world where everyone is unique yet connected, different yet equal. It's the joy of learning from each other, growing together, and building a more inclusive, equitable, and compassionate world.

The joy of unity in diversity isn't just a lofty ideal. It's a practical necessity for our interconnected world. Our diversity is our strength, our wealth, and our promise. It's what makes us innovative, resilient, and vibrant. By embracing our diversity and fostering inclusion, we can create societies that are more understanding, more harmonious, and more just.

So let's celebrate the beautiful mosaic of our world. Let's appreciate our unique pieces and our shared picture. Let's champion diversity, challenge stereotypes, promote inclusion, and practice allyship. Let's savor the joy of unity in diversity and the promise of a better world.

Chapter 14: Power of Kindness: Making the World Better, One Smile at a Time

66. Understanding Kindness

Kindness is a virtue that is at once simple and profound. It is the act of extending empathy, love, and understanding to others, without asking for anything in return. At its core, kindness is a way of connecting on a human level, of acknowledging the essential dignity and worth of every person we encounter. But this simple act has a depth and power that can often be overlooked.

In the world we live in, actions that gain the most attention are often those that are grand, bold, and dramatic. Yet the quiet power of kindness, gently exercised in small ways every day, can have a transformative effect on individuals and communities. It is the accumulation of these small acts of generosity, care, and understanding that can build bridges, heal wounds, and create a more compassionate world.

A smile, a friendly word, a moment taken to listen, can mean so much to someone who is feeling down or isolated. These small gestures of kindness can affirm their worth, validate their experiences, and lighten their burdens. And they cost nothing but a moment of attention and a spark of empathy.

67. The Power of Small Acts

But how can small acts of kindness change the world? It's all about the ripple effect. Just as a small stone can create large ripples when it's dropped in a pond, so can our actions influence those around us. Every act of kindness can inspire and encourage others to be kinder, creating a ripple effect that can spread out and touch countless lives.

Imagine if you helped someone and they, inspired by your kindness, went on to help someone else. And that person did the same. And so on. That's how one act of kindness can multiply and grow, touching more lives than you could ever know.

This ripple effect can create a culture of kindness, where people feel appreciated, connected, and empowered. It can foster mutual respect, empathy, and collaboration. It can counteract negativity, division, and isolation. That's the transformative power of small acts of kindness.

68. Being Kind to Yourself

Yet kindness should not only be directed outward, but also inward. Being kind to yourself is just as important as being kind to others. It's about treating yourself with the same love, respect, and compassion that you would offer to others. It's about acknowledging your worth, honoring your needs, and caring for your well-being.

Self-kindness can involve giving yourself a break when you're stressed, forgiving yourself when you make a mistake, or treating yourself when you need a boost. It can involve respecting your limits, celebrating your achievements, and nurturing your dreams.

Remember, you can't pour from an empty cup. By being kind to yourself, you refill your cup and ensure that you have the energy, resilience, and joy to be kind to others. So let's cultivate self-kindness as diligently as we cultivate kindness to others.

69. Encouraging Kindness in Others

While it's important to be kind, it's also important to encourage kindness in others. By modeling kindness, recognizing kindness, and advocating for kindness, you can inspire and empower others to be kinder. This can help create a more compassionate, understanding, and harmonious world.

Modeling kindness involves leading by example. By being kind in your interactions, you can show others how to be kind and demonstrate the benefits of kindness. Recognizing kindness involves acknowledging and appreciating when others are kind. This can reinforce their positive behavior and motivate them to be even kinder. Advocating for kindness involves promoting the importance of kindness in your communities and societies. This can help cultivate a culture of kindness and make kindness a norm.

70. The Joy of Kindness

Ultimately, kindness brings a profound joy: the joy of connecting deeply with others, of making a positive difference, and of becoming a better person. It's the joy of seeing a smile light up someone's face, of hearing a heartfelt thank you, of feeling a warm glow in your heart. It's the joy that comes from knowing that you've touched a life, eased a burden, or brightened a day.

Moreover, kindness can also enhance your own well-being. Studies show that being kind can boost your mood, lower your stress, and even improve your health. It can give you a sense of purpose, increase your self-esteem, and foster your personal growth.

So let's unleash the power of kindness. Let's light up the world with our smiles, our words, our actions. Let's spread the ripples of kindness far and wide. Let's transform our world, one act of kindness at a time.

Chapter 15: Love, Crushes, and Everything in Between: Navigating Your First Relationships

71. Understanding Your Feelings

In the grand tapestry of life, the threads of love and relationships weave some of the most vivid, complex, and emotional patterns. As a young girl standing on the threshold of adolescence, you may begin to experience new and confusing feelings for others— a classmate, a friend, or even a celebrity. Understanding these feelings is the first step in navigating the world of love and relationships.

When you have a crush, your heart might flutter every time you see that person, or you might find yourself daydreaming about them in the middle of class. Crushes are a normal part of growing up— they're how we explore our feelings and learn about attraction. While they can be filled with joy and excitement, they can also bring confusion and anxiety, especially if it's your first time experiencing such feelings. It's important to remember that what you're feeling is completely normal and that everyone experiences these emotions at some point in their life.

You may feel an overwhelming urge to be liked or loved by your crush, and it's normal to want these feelings reciprocated. However, keep in mind that not every crush leads to a relationship and that's okay. You're learning more about yourself— your likes, your dislikes, your values, and your feelings— and that is invaluable. You're also learning that it's okay to have feelings for someone, even if they don't feel the same way.

72. The Importance of Communication

A crucial aspect of navigating your first relationships and crushes is communication. It's important to express your feelings honestly and clearly. If you like someone, consider telling them how you feel. It can be scary, but remember, being courageous doesn't mean you aren't afraid— it means you go for it anyway because it's important to you.

But communication isn't just about expressing your feelings; it's also about listening and understanding the feelings of others. If someone tells you they have feelings for you, take the time to listen to them and respond with kindness, even if you don't feel the same way. And if you're on the other end, respect their feelings if they don't reciprocate yours.

Additionally, understand that good communication also means setting and respecting boundaries. Just because you have strong feelings for someone doesn't mean you're ready for all aspects of a relationship. It's okay to take things slow and communicate your comfort levels.

73. Dealing with Rejection

Rejection can be hard. It can feel like a blow to your self-esteem, and it can cause a lot of pain. However, it's important to remember that everyone experiences rejection at some point, and it doesn't define your worth or desirability.

Rejection often has less to do with you and more to do with the other person's feelings, circumstances, or preferences. It doesn't mean you're not good enough; it just means you weren't a good match for that person at this time. And that's okay— not everyone we have feelings for is meant to be a good match for us.

When you face rejection, allow yourself to feel your emotions without judgment. It's okay to feel sad, hurt, or disappointed. Reach out to supportive friends or family members and share your feelings. Engage in activities that you enjoy and that make you feel good about yourself. In time, you'll heal and be ready to try again.

74. Healthy vs Unhealthy Relationships

As you start navigating the realm of relationships, it's crucial to understand the difference between healthy and unhealthy ones. Healthy relationships are based on mutual respect, trust, honesty, support, equality, and good communication. They make you feel good about yourself and bring joy and enrichment to your life.

Unhealthy relationships, on the other hand, involve control, manipulation, dishonesty, disrespect, excessive jealousy, and abuse (physical, emotional, or sexual). They bring pain, confusion, and fear, and they erode your self-esteem and happiness.

Always remember that you deserve to be in a relationship that makes you feel loved, respected, and valued, not one that makes you feel unimportant, scared, or bad about yourself. Listen to your gut feelings, and if something doesn't feel right, it probably isn't.

75. First Breakups

First breakups can be challenging and painful. Whether it was your decision or not, ending a relationship can bring feelings of loss, sadness, and confusion. But just like with rejection, it's important to remember that breakups are a normal part of life, and they don't define your worth or your ability to find love again.

It's okay to grieve the end of a relationship. Allow yourself to feel your emotions and process your loss. But also remember to take care of yourself. Reach out to supportive friends and family, engage in activities you enjoy, and practice self-care. Use this time to reflect on what you've learned from the relationship and how you've grown.

Remember, it's okay to take your time to heal and to be single. Being single is an opportunity to learn more about yourself, explore your interests, and cultivate your strengths. It's a time to build a strong foundation of self-love and self-respect, which will help you build healthier and happier relationships in the future.

Chapter 16: Dollars and Sense: Smart Money Habits for Young Girls

76. Understanding Money: The Basics

Understanding money—what it is, how it works, and how to manage it—is a fundamental life skill. Money is a tool that can provide us with the things we need and want, but it is also a resource that must be managed wisely. So, where do we start?

The basics of understanding money revolve around knowing how to earn, save, spend, and donate. When you earn money, whether it's from an allowance, a part-time job, or birthday gifts, you're gaining a resource that you have control over. How you choose to use it can have a big impact on your life now and in the future. When you save money, you're setting it aside for future use. This could be for a specific goal like buying a new book or for unforeseen needs like replacing a broken bicycle. Spending is when you exchange money for goods or services. This is often the most visible aspect of money, but it's only part of the picture. Lastly, donating is about giving some of your resources to help others or causes that are important to you.

77. Earning Money: Opportunities and Responsibilities

As a young girl, there may be limited opportunities to earn money. However, there are still ways you can start to understand the concept of earning. Perhaps you get an allowance for doing chores, or maybe you can earn money by babysitting, dog walking, or even selling crafts or lemonade.

Earning money provides not only a source of income but also a sense of responsibility and empowerment. You begin to understand the value of work and the satisfaction of earning your own money. It's a critical lesson in self-reliance and responsibility that lays the groundwork for financial independence in adulthood. It's important to learn that money isn't just given; it's earned, and this process requires effort, responsibility, and often patience.

78. Saving Money: Why It's Important and How to Do It

Saving money is a fundamental aspect of financial literacy. When you save, you set money aside for future needs or goals. This could be anything from saving up for a new book you want to read, to planning for larger future expenses like college.

Saving is essential because it allows you to have money available for unexpected costs and helps you reach your financial goals. It also teaches patience and delayed gratification—when you want something, you may have to wait and save up for it rather than getting it immediately.

You can start saving by setting aside a certain amount of money regularly. Even if it's just a small amount, the habit of saving is what's important. Consider having a separate place to keep your savings, like a piggy bank or a separate compartment in your wallet, so you're not tempted to spend it.

79. Spending Wisely: Making Informed Decisions

Spending money can be fun and satisfying, but it's important to make sure you're spending wisely. This means making informed decisions about when to spend money and what to spend it on. Before you make a purchase, ask yourself: Do I really need this? Is it worth the cost? Are there other things I'd rather save my money for?

Comparison shopping is another good way to spend wisely. This means looking at different stores or websites to see where you can get the best price for the item you want. Also, consider the quality of the items you're buying—sometimes, spending a bit more money for a better-quality item that will last longer is a smarter decision than buying a cheaper item that will need to be replaced quickly.

It's also important to understand the concept of "wants" vs "needs." Needs are things you must have to survive and function—like food, clothing, and a place to live. Wants are things you'd like to have but don't necessarily need. Learning to prioritize needs over wants is a key aspect of spending wisely.

80. Giving Back: The Role of Donating

Finally, part of being financially responsible involves giving back. This means donating some of your money to causes that are important to you. Donating money helps you understand that, while money is a tool for buying things you want and need, it's also a way to help others and make a positive impact in the world.

Donating isn't just for the rich. Even a small amount can make a big difference to someone in need or to an organization that relies on donations. Plus, giving to others not only helps them, but it also gives you a sense of satisfaction and fulfillment.

When deciding where to donate, think about what causes are important to you. Do you love animals? Consider donating to a local animal shelter. Are you passionate about helping people in need? Maybe you could give to a food bank or a charity that helps children in poor countries. Do your research to make sure the organizations you're donating to are reputable and that the majority of their funds go directly to their cause.

Understanding and managing money may seem intimidating at first, but it's a journey. The more you learn and the more experience you gain, the more comfortable and confident you'll become. Remember, smart money habits aren't just about having money—they're about managing it wisely and using it in ways that align with your values and goals.

Chapter 17: My Crazy, Beautiful Family: Dealing with Family Dynamics

81. Understanding Family Dynamics: The Unique Puzzle That Makes Your Family

Family dynamics are the patterns of interaction and relationships among family members. Each family is a unique puzzle, with each member being a distinctive piece that contributes to the overall picture. Some families are loud and chaotic, while others are quiet and orderly. Some families have lots of members living under the same roof, while others are small and tight-knit.

Understanding your family dynamics involves recognizing the roles each family member plays, the relationships between family members, and how these relationships and roles shape the way your family functions. It also involves understanding that family dynamics can change over time due to various factors such as aging, shifts in the household, and life events. Learning about family dynamics can help you better understand why your family interacts the way it does and can also help you navigate potential challenges more effectively.

82. Accepting Differences: Respecting Individuality Within Your Family

Even within a family, individuals can be vastly different. A family could be a melting pot of personalities, interests, and quirks. You may find yourself wondering how you ended up in such a diverse group of individuals. And yet, these differences are precisely what makes your family unique and special.

Recognizing, accepting, and respecting these differences is a critical part of maintaining harmony within your family. It involves understanding that everyone has different ways of thinking, feeling, and behaving, and that these differences are not necessarily good or bad, just different. Remember, it's okay to disagree with your family members or not understand why they do certain things.

What's important is that you respect their right to be themselves, just as they should respect your right to be you.

83. Navigating Family Conflicts: Learning How to Communicate and Compromise

No family is without conflict. Disagreements are a normal part of any relationship, and family relationships are no exception. Whether it's a squabble over who gets the last piece of cake or a deeper disagreement about family rules or decisions, conflicts are inevitable.

However, it's not the conflict itself that's the problem—it's how you handle it. Learning to communicate effectively and compromise is key to navigating family conflicts. This means expressing your feelings and thoughts clearly and respectfully, listening to and trying to understand others' perspectives, and working together to find a solution that everyone can live with. It's important to remember that the goal is not necessarily to "win" the argument but to resolve the conflict in a way that maintains the relationship and respects everyone involved.

84. Roles in the Family: Understanding and Navigating Them

Every family member plays a role in the family, whether it's the responsible one, the peacemaker, the rebel, the baby of the family, or any other role. These roles are often influenced by factors such as birth order, personality, and family expectations.

Understanding your role and the roles of others in your family can give you insight into the dynamics of your family and why family members behave the way they do. However, it's also important to remember that these roles are not fixed—you're not confined to the role you've been assigned, and you have the ability to change and grow. If you feel pigeonholed into a certain role or are unhappy with the dynamics in your family, it can be helpful to communicate your feelings with your family or seek guidance from a trusted adult or professional.

85. Growing Together and Apart: Accepting Change and Evolution in Your Family

As time goes on, families change and evolve. Children grow up, parents age, family members come and go, and life events can significantly alter the family dynamic. These changes can be bittersweet and sometimes challenging to accept.

However, change is a natural part of life, and it's no different for your family. As you and your family members grow and change, the dynamics within your family will shift and evolve as well. Embracing these changes and viewing them as opportunities for growth and learning can help you navigate them more effectively. Remember, it's okay to outgrow certain family roles or traditions, and it's okay for relationships within your family to evolve. What's important is that you continue to love and support each other through these changes.

Your family, with all its unique dynamics, conflicts, roles, and changes, is a significant part of your life. While it may not always be easy, learning to navigate your family dynamics can lead to a greater understanding of yourself and others, enhance your communication and problem-solving skills, and contribute to your overall personal growth. Remember, it's the crazy, beautiful uniqueness of your family that makes it truly special.

Chapter 18: Making a Difference: Understanding the Joy of Helping Others

86. The Power of One: How You Can Make a Difference

Often, we underestimate the impact one person can make. We might believe that we are too young or too insignificant to effect real change. However, history is full of examples of individuals who made a significant difference in their communities or even the world. Remember, change often starts small, and every person can contribute to making the world a better place.

In this section, we'll explore different ways you can make a difference, whether it's through volunteering, advocating for a cause you believe in, or even just helping out a neighbor or friend. Remember, making a difference is not about grand gestures; it's about the small, everyday actions that add up to create big change. By understanding that you hold this power within you, you can begin to see the potential for positive change you have in your community and the world.

87. The Gift of Giving: Discovering the Joy in Helping Others

There's a unique joy that comes from helping others, a sense of fulfillment and happiness that can't be gained from anything else. This is because giving is not just about the recipient; it's also about the giver. When you help others, you're also helping yourself. You're cultivating empathy, building character, and expanding your understanding of different people and their experiences.

This section will explore the many ways in which helping others can enrich your life. Whether you're giving your time, resources, or skills, every act of giving can have a profound impact on your wellbeing and happiness. And as you discover the joy of giving, you may find that the more you give, the more you receive in return.

88. Volunteering: Giving Your Time and Talents to Serve Others

Volunteering is one of the most direct ways to make a difference in your community. Whether you choose to volunteer at a local food bank, tutor children after school, clean up your local park, or help out at an animal shelter, there are countless ways to lend your time and talents to causes that matter to you.

In this section, we'll discuss how to find volunteering opportunities that align with your interests and passions, how to make the most of your volunteering experience, and how to balance volunteering with your other responsibilities. Remember, volunteering is not just about what you can offer; it's also an opportunity to learn, grow, and connect with others in your community.

89. Advocacy: Standing Up for What You Believe In

Advocacy is about using your voice to make a difference. It's about standing up for what you believe in and working to bring about the change you want to see. Whether it's advocating for more funding for your school, speaking out against bullying, or rallying for environmental conservation, every voice matters and can contribute to the cause.

This section will provide an overview of what advocacy involves, how you can get involved in advocacy, and how to effectively use your voice for change. It will also discuss the importance of informed advocacy—that is, understanding the issues you're advocating for, knowing the change you want to see, and being aware of the most effective ways to bring about that change.

90. The Ripple Effect: Seeing the Impact of Your Actions

When you throw a stone into a pond, it creates ripples that spread out far beyond the point of impact. Similarly, every action you take can have far-reaching effects. This is known as the ripple effect. When you help someone, not only are you impacting that person, but you're also potentially impacting every other person they interact with.

In this section, we'll explore the ripple effect in the context of making a difference. We'll discuss how even small actions can have a big impact and how your efforts to help others can create a ripple effect of positivity in your community and beyond. As you begin to see the impact of your actions, you may find a newfound motivation to continue making a difference, creating a continuous cycle of positivity and change.

Making a difference is about more than just helping others; it's about becoming a more empathetic, compassionate, and proactive individual. It's about realizing your power to effect change and taking steps to use that power for good. And as you embark on this journey of making a difference, you'll discover the profound joy and fulfillment that comes from giving, serving, advocating, and seeing the impact of your actions. Remember, no act of kindness, no matter how small, is ever wasted.

Chapter 19: Self-Love Sundays: The Importance of Self-Care and Relaxation

91. Understanding Self-Care: More Than Just Bubble Baths

Self-care, as you may have heard, is crucial for your overall well-being. However, it's more than just pampering yourself with luxurious bubble baths or indulging in your favorite treats. It's about taking care of your mental, emotional, and physical health. It's about taking time to rest, rejuvenate and replenish yourself in all areas of life.

In this section, we will explore what self-care truly means and how it goes beyond just physical pampering. We'll discuss the many dimensions of self-care, from maintaining a healthy lifestyle and managing stress to nurturing positive relationships and cultivating a growth mindset. Furthermore, we'll explore the importance of self-care in maintaining balance in your life and how neglecting self-care can lead to burnout and other health issues.

92. Establishing Your Self-Care Routine: A Ritual of Love

Having a regular self-care routine can help ensure that you're taking care of your well-being on a consistent basis. However, your self-care routine should be more than just a list of tasks to complete. Instead, think of it as a ritual of love - a time dedicated to nurturing yourself and your needs.

In this section, we'll provide guidance on how to establish a self-care routine that resonates with you. We'll discuss how to identify activities that nourish your mind, body, and soul, and how to make these activities a regular part of your life. From creating a relaxing bedtime routine to setting aside time for hobbies you love, we'll explore different ways to create a self-care routine that truly serves you.

93. Mindful Moments: Incorporating Mindfulness into Your Self-Care Routine

Mindfulness is a powerful tool for self-care. It's about being fully present in the moment, paying attention to your thoughts, feelings, and sensations without judgment. By practicing mindfulness, you can cultivate a deeper awareness of yourself and your needs, making your self-care routine more effective.

In this part of the chapter, we'll discuss how to incorporate mindfulness into your self-care routine. We'll explore different mindfulness practices, such as mindful breathing, mindful eating, and mindful walking, and how these practices can help you relax, reduce stress, and enhance your overall well-being. Remember, mindfulness is not about achieving a state of constant calm or happiness. Instead, it's about observing what is happening within you and around you with an open and nonjudgmental attitude.

94. Self-Care and Relationships: Taking Care of Your Social Well-Being

While self-care often involves solitary activities, taking care of your social well-being is also an essential part of self-care. This can involve cultivating healthy relationships, setting boundaries, and taking time to connect with the people who matter to you.

In this section, we'll delve into the role of relationships in self-care. We'll talk about the importance of nurturing relationships that uplift and support you, how to establish and maintain boundaries that protect your well-being, and how to prioritize meaningful social interactions in your self-care routine. Whether it's spending time with family, catching up with friends, or enjoying some quality time with your pet, taking care of your social well-being can greatly enhance your overall self-care routine.

95. Overcoming Challenges in Self-Care: When Taking Care of Yourself Feels Like a Chore

Self-care is meant to be a loving act of kindness towards yourself. However, there can be times when it feels like another item on your to-do list, a chore that adds to your stress rather than alleviating it. When this happens, it's important to remember that self-care is not about perfection or ticking off a checklist.

This part of the chapter will provide guidance on how to navigate challenges in your self-care journey. We'll talk about how to make your self-care routine flexible and adaptable, how to overcome feelings of guilt or selfishness associated with self-care, and how to find joy and satisfaction in taking care of yourself. Remember, self-care is a journey, not a destination. It's about being kind to yourself, honoring your needs, and cultivating a loving relationship with yourself.

As you embark on your self-care journey, remember that self-care is an act of self-love. It's about acknowledging your worth and taking steps to nurture your well-being. By prioritizing self-care and incorporating it into your daily life, you can create a foundation for a healthier, happier, and more balanced life. So go ahead, dedicate your Sundays (and any day that ends in 'y') to self-love and see how it changes your life.

Chapter 20: Ready, Set, Grow! Preparing for the Exciting World of Adulthood

96. Embracing Change: The Journey from Girlhood to Womanhood

Transitioning from girlhood to womanhood can be a thrilling yet challenging journey. This is a period in your life when you undergo significant changes, both physically and emotionally. Embracing these changes and the growth that comes with them is a crucial part of preparing for adulthood.

In this section, we will discuss the changes that take place as you transition into adulthood, and how to embrace these changes with confidence and grace. We'll cover topics ranging from the physical changes brought on by puberty to the emotional and psychological growth you'll experience during this time. We'll also delve into how these changes can shape your identity and influence your personal journey to adulthood. Remember, this is a period of your life when you get to explore, discover, and shape who you are and who you want to be.

97. Skills for Independence: Learning to Stand on Your Own

As you transition into adulthood, developing skills for independence becomes increasingly important. From managing your finances and maintaining a healthy lifestyle to nurturing relationships and making sound decisions, these skills will help you navigate the world of adulthood with confidence.

This part of the chapter will provide practical advice and guidance on developing skills for independence. We'll cover a range of topics, including money management, time management, health and wellness, and relationship skills. We'll also explore the importance of critical thinking and decision-making skills, and how you can develop these skills to make informed decisions that align with your values and goals.

98. Navigating Relationships in Adulthood: From Family to Friendship and Love

Relationships in adulthood can be complex and multi-faceted, encompassing familial relationships, friendships, and romantic relationships. As you enter adulthood, you may find yourself encountering new challenges and experiences in your relationships.

In this section, we'll explore the dynamics of relationships in adulthood. We'll provide guidance on nurturing healthy and fulfilling relationships with family, friends, and romantic partners. We'll also delve into the topics of setting boundaries, expressing your needs and feelings, and managing conflicts in relationships. Whether you're dealing with changes in your family dynamics, building new friendships, or navigating your first serious romantic relationship, this section will provide you with valuable insights to help you navigate the complexities of adult relationships.

99. Career Exploration: Finding Your Path in the World of Work

One of the most exciting and daunting aspects of adulthood is entering the world of work. Whether you're planning to go to university, start an apprenticeship, or jump straight into the workforce, it's important to explore your career options and find a path that aligns with your interests, values, and aspirations.

In this part of the chapter, we'll discuss the process of career exploration. We'll provide guidance on identifying your interests and strengths, researching different career options, and making informed career decisions. We'll also cover the importance of developing a strong work ethic and resilience, and how these qualities can help you succeed in the world of work.

100. Becoming Your Best Self: A Lifelong Journey of Growth and Self-Discovery

As you prepare for adulthood, it's important to remember that this is just the beginning of your journey. Adulthood is not a destination, but a journey of growth and self-discovery. It's about becoming your best self, living a life that aligns with your values, and continuously growing and evolving.

This concluding section of the chapter will provide inspiration and guidance on becoming your best self as you enter adulthood. We'll explore the concept of personal growth and how you can cultivate a mindset of continuous learning and self-improvement. We'll also discuss the importance of self-reflection and introspection in your journey of self-discovery.

As you embark on your journey to adulthood, remember that it's okay to make mistakes, change your mind, and take detours. Adulthood is not about having all the answers, but about exploring, learning, and growing. So get ready, set your sights on the future, and embark on your exciting journey of growth and self-discovery.

101. The Never-Ending Story: Writing Your Own Chapters

As we approach the conclusion of this book, remember that this is not the end of your unique narrative. In fact, it's just the beginning of many more intriguing chapters yet to be inscribed. You are about to step into the expansive world of adulthood, and it's important to realize that your personal growth and transformation is an ongoing journey, not a destination.

Every day presents a fresh page in your life's book, an opportunity to script your experiences, dreams, setbacks, and victories. You are the one in control. You are the author of your life, the creator of your destiny, and the architect of your dreams.

The first segment of this closing chapter will discuss the value of continuous learning and personal evolution. Adaptability and resilience, two essential traits for encountering new experiences and overcoming challenges, will be a focal point.

We will also talk about the significance of being present in your life, of embracing the 'now', and how each moment contributes to your overall growth. Realizing that each day and each moment offers new opportunities for expansion and understanding, opens up a whole new perspective on life.

In the following section, we will explore the importance of remaining true to your core self and leading an authentic life. As you grow and evolve, you may find your beliefs, values, and passions shifting. This is a natural part of life. Embrace it. However, remember that change does not imply losing your essence; rather, it indicates an evolution towards a more refined version of yourself.

Next, we delve into the realm of uncertainty. The transition into adulthood is not a linear path. It is filled with unexpected detours, exhilarating experiences, and formidable challenges. A degree of apprehension about what the future holds is expected. However, uncertainty is not inherently negative. It's an integral part of life that shapes your character and moulds your spirit.

Finally, we explore the notion of balance. Achieving equilibrium in various aspects of life is key to maintaining harmony. Knowing when to push forward and when to step back, when to relentlessly chase your dreams and when to pause and appreciate the journey forms a vital part of this balance. Insights on maintaining this equilibrium, such as finding the right blend between work and leisure, striving for improvement and accepting oneself as is, giving and receiving, among others, will be discussed.

As we draw this book to a close, remember that your narrative is a perpetual work in progress, filled with new paths, experiences, and life lessons. You are about to embark on an exciting journey filled with limitless opportunities for growth, love, happiness, and self-expression. So, as you step into the vibrant world of adulthood, take a deep breath, embrace the journey, and remember: this is your story. Your life is a book with numerous chapters yet to be written. Take the pen in your hand and let your unique narrative unfold.

© Copyright

Silas Meadowlark - 2023

Printed in Great Britain
by Amazon